Faithing It

BOOK 2

JONES-WHITFIELD

Books may be purchased in quantity by contacting the author by email lorrainewhitfield7@gmail.com, or by visiting www.shesoarsllc.com.

"The weapons of our warfare are not carnal but mighty in God for pulling down strongholds." — *2 Corinthians 10:4*

Scriptures come from the King James version, New Living Translation, New Kings James Version, NASV, ESV versions of the Bible.

First Edition 2020

Table of Contents

When Ye Pray

"And when ye stand praying, forgive, if ye have ought against any: that your Father also which is in heaven may forgive you your trespasses."

— Mark 11:24-25

"Confess your faults one to another, and pray one for another, that ye may be healed. The effectual fervent prayer of a righteous man availeth much."

— James 5:16

We want prayers to be effective so much that we focus on the results of our prayers that we know that it was God and not ourselves. We must make sure our prayers are in line with God's will.

"And this is the confidence that we have in him, that, if we ask any thing according to his will, he heareth us: And if we know that he hear us, whatsoever we ask, we know that we have the petitions that we desired of him.

— 1 John 5:14-15

If you are sick and need for spiritual healing, praying these scriptures on healing will help increase your faith.

Read and meditate on them daily, morning, noon and night. Trust in the Lord with all of your heart and do not lean to your understanding but walk by faith and not by sight.

The word of God will increase our faith to believe, but it will be a reminder that when all those aches and pains come, that Jesus took sicknesses and diseases with Him to the cross when He died. Sickness and disease went to the cross with Jesus an, therefore, we are healed. (Isaiah 53:5).

"So shall my word be that goeth forth out of my mouth: it shall not return unto me void, but it shall accomplish that which I please, and it shall prosper in the thing whereto I sent it."

— Isaiah 55:11

Lorraine Jones-Whitfield 2020

Introduction

May you find blessing, inspiration and lots of faith in this journal to help you understand the word of God and your faith. May God bless you to discover you as you discover new ways to fulfill your potential as a believer in Christ

Each day offers scripture and a space to share your thoughts about the word of God to help you to tune into your actions and attitude into what God wants you to accomplish in your everyday life. Choose a practical action and claim the promises of God through His word and by faith. He will never leave you nor forsake you. Just abide in Him.

"I will speak of excellent things, and from the opening of my lips will come right things"

— Proverbs 8:6

Let's Faith It 2 with Gratitude …. Along with my journal, at the end of this there will be a place where you can use it for your own daily personal journal. This way you can pour out your heart unto the Lord and by faith, you can journal your day. Thoughts and thanksgiving to the Lord. The goal is to strengthen your faith and to build an unshakable relationship with God. By faithing we are trusting God with it all.

"Seek ye the Lord while he may be found, call ye upon him while he is near."

— Isaiah 55:6

Please enjoy this journal/workbook and write, read, pray, and meditate as you read. It deserves a place in our lives. Coloring sheets are included for extra doodling and for peace of mind. Please enjoy as you learn more about the Lord and His goodness.

"Give unto the LORD the glory due unto his name; worship the LORD in the beauty of holiness."

— Psalm 29:2

In His Service
Raine

"I don't care what you're going through, I don't care what you're facing until you change your mind about it, you can't change anything else."

— TD. JAKES

Acknowledgments

Thank you for your support and encouragement and for reading my book, Personal Journal: Let's Faith It. And now you will get the honor to work in my workbook/ journal Lets Faith It 2. In this journal, we'll walk in faith and gratitude through the promises of God. Some things in life seem impossible, but through God all things are possible. God can go places we can't. He is the ultimate healer, way-maker, and deliverer. He has great things in store for us.

I am thankful for my storms and the situations I've had to endure throughout my life. They have been hard, and some may not understand how I can be so thankful. Well, I would not be where I am today if it were not for Him. For many years, I prayed for God to bless me in certain areas of life, and I can now see those prayers come to pass. By faithing it and being thankful, I made it through. So, my friends, I thank God for your support and believing in me. I am thankful for my friends, who helped and encouraged me as I write and get my books out there and my grandkids especially. They are my inspiration as I do what I do along with my children.

I'm also grateful for my son, Chris, who edited them and made sure they were ready to be published and most of all my husband, Carlton, who endure the toughest times without me while I am writing and getting these things out for Gods glory. I am thankful for his prayers and patience and all the love he shared as I endured.

I want you to open your hearts and minds and Lets Faith It 2 with me. God brought me through a bad car accident involving a tractor trailer without crushing me, and I praise and thank Him. I give Him thanks for delivering me from a wheelchair, a hospital bed, an extensive surgery, a walker, and a pair of crutches (and I can go on and on). He said, "Arise (RISE) and take up your bed and walk." I took that scripture as it was me and did it exactly. I thank God for taking me through. When I read His word, I believe it and my faith does not waver. Just know that God can do all He says and more (Ephesians 3:20).

In His Service
Lorraine Jones-Whitfield

Now Faith

"Now faith is the substance of things hoped for, the evidence of things not seen."

— Hebrews 11:1

Do we have the faith to believe the impossible? Do we have that "now faith" to believe in our healing? Do we have that faith to know God is able? No matter what our situation looks like or feels like, just know God is in it.

In the book of Job, we see God allowed Satan to test Job, but was told not to harm him in any way. God has that hedge of protection around us, but we can't see it in the natural. God is the beginning and the ending of our Faith.

"Have faith in God," Jesus answered. "Truly I tell you, if anyone says to this mountain, 'Go, throw yourself into the sea,' and does not doubt in their heart but believes that what they say will happen, it will be done for them. Therefore, I tell you, whatever you ask for in prayer, believe that you have received it, and it will be yours."

— Mark 11:22-24

Do we believe the impossible? "Now faith" is the assurance to know that whatever God says we can do or whatever we need in life it is done. It is because we asked Him and believed that mountain to be moved. There was a time I had a goiter in my throat and the doctors said it was cancerous without testing it. It got bigger to the point that I couldn't swallow and every time I ate or drank, I would choke. The doctors told my husband the next step would be to surgically remove the goiter and we did. That meant that my thyroid would have to be removed and I would take thyroid medication for the rest of my life. To me, that would be a blessing because that meant no cancer. The surgery took place and they removed the thyroid and the goiter. Hallelujah! The biopsy came back and no cancer. God is good. Did I believe for the impossible? Yes. I trusted God in my most trying time. He came through once again. He showed Himself strong and I was cancer free. Do I believe God for my healing? Yes, I do because He has healed me in the situation with the goiter, through a car accident, and with fibroid tumors and more. I totally trust Him in all things.

"But he was pierced for our transgressions, he was crushed for our iniquities; the punishment that brought us peace was on him, and by his wounds we are healed."

— Isaiah 53:5

I take God's words and eat them like food. I believe it, I breath it, and bank on it. He has never failed me yet. He won't because His word is true. Do we have that faith to know God is able?

"God is not human, that he should lie, not a human being changes his mind. Does he speak and then not act? Does he promise and not fulfill?"

— Numbers 23:19

Whatever He says He will do that, He will. God is qualified and more than able to do everything he says and more. God has supplied when we could not see a way out. He has opened doors where there were no doors. We had so many needs, but God has fulfilled every one of them and has never let us down. So, you see, I can trust God in the good and bad times and in all my seasons. He is my shepherd I shall not have a need (Psalm 23).

God has delivered me from so many things in my life and never have I doubted that He wouldn't bring me out. By Faith He created this world. By Faith Sarah had a baby at her old age. By faith God parted the Red Sea and the people crossed over on dry land. By faith he healed the woman with the issue of blood, opened the blinded eyes, and raised Lazarus from the dead after four long days. By faith Noah built an ark and didn't know if he would see rain but he followed Gods instruction, and by faith He created you and me. So, there is nothing impossible for God to do. We just need to follow His plan. He has given us the instructions and it's up to us to be obedient. He has a plan for us and therefore we must believe that He can and that He will. We must trust what we don't see and believe for a great outcome.

"Without faith, it's impossible to please God."

— Hebrews 11:6

"Faith, it's all about believing, you don't know how it will happen, but you know it will."

— Unknown

Day 1

Fearless Faith

Faith without works is dead

I can remember when I was about to move to Wilson, NC, and there was so much to do after the decision was made. I began to pray and all I know is that my emotions were all over the place. There were so many things to do and so many boxes to pack and contacting so many people and places as we were about to move to another land. Letting go was hard and leaving our hometown was even harder. I had to leave my dad and my siblings behind. But in my heart, I knew it was time to move on. Isaiah 43:19- God said he would be doing a new thing and I was excited in my New. The area would be new, people would be new, the house would be new, and my life would be too. I was nervous about the transition, but i was excited at the same time.

So, we began to pray by faith and God answered and opened doors. Trusting Him became easy to me because I live by my own crazy faith. We pitched our tent as Abraham did, and we trusted God on this journey. Genesis 12:1-3 became real to my husband and me at different times. We hung on to that word and trusted God is doing just what he said. He would make our name great and, do a new thing and make a way in the wilderness and rivers in the desert. He can do exceedingly and abundantly above all that we ask or think according to the power that worketh in us, (Ephesians 3:20) that we ask or think according to the power. His word is right all by itself. God showed us that he will do for us not only more than we ask and our desire when we pray. He has shown us that he can do anything farther than our imagination could perceive.

By FAITH! When you don't see the way, trust the way because His word says that He will give you water in the wilderness because in Isaiah the word says, "Behold I WILL DO A NEW THING" (Isaiah 43:19). He will make a way in the wilderness and rivers in the desert. So yes, I will trust and believe the almighty God. FAITH makes things happen.

This is how Lets Faith it "The personal Journal was born and then "Faithing IT "and "Kids Faith It Too" came along. We live by faith and not by sight. We walk on this earth knowing and believing exactly what God said he would do and more. I am trusting God to open more doors for us and for many others. God's word will not come back empty. It will accomplish just what it is supposed to (Isaiah 55:11).

Day 1 _____

Scripture and Notes

_____
_____
_____
_____
_____
_____
_____
_____
_____
_____
_____
_____
_____
_____
_____
_____
_____
_____
_____
_____
_____
_____
_____
_____
_____
_____
_____
_____
_____
_____
_____
_____
_____

Day 2

The Beauty of Faithing it

Commit thy way unto the LORD; trust also in him, and he shall bring it to pass.

— Psalm 37:5

Many people have their own concept of faith, but the only true faith is biblical. Faith is the assurance that God can do whatever He wants to and that He is working in your favor. His word does not come back void, but it accomplishes just what it is sent to do (Isaiah 55:11). Without faith, there is no way we can please God. His thoughts are not ours and His ways aren't either because they are much higher than ours.

There are many levels of faith and Christian faith is based on God's promises rather than feelings or visible things. Great faith holds fast regardless of how it appears outwardly. Spending that quality time with God and reading His word will increase our faith. The one who truly believes and has faith will act. God's word will perfect that assurance and his request will be granted.

> *"For as many as are led by the Spirit of God, they are the sons of God. For ye have not received the spirit of bondage again to fear; but ye have received the Spirit of adoption, whereby we cry, Abba, Father. The Spirit itself beareth witness with our spirit, that we are the children of God."*

— Romans 8:14-32

When my mom passed, I didn't understand why after I had prayed with unwavering faith. I just knew that He would answer and by faith, He would heal. Well, He did heal cancer but I didn't pray for the healing of her heart because I didn't know that her heart was struggling, nor did I know that between chemo or diabetes her heart had been weakened. Life has its strange ways, but God knows us all.

God worked it the way that I asked, and He healed her in the way she wanted to be healed. She was ready to move on and she trusted God through it all. I may not have understood the process, but I trusted God in His plan. When I would look at her weak and lifeless body , she would whisper the prayers in her heart. She fought to live but God knew what was up ahead and therefore we had to trust His plan.

Because of my faith in God had caused her faith to increase. We would pray and anoint her body with oil and believe for God to move, and He did in many ways.She also began to believe in her healing and deliverance. I watched her move out on faith and she totally tusted God for the outcome. God did heal that cancer as the doctor said ,but it was the heart and because she wanted to leave and move to the heavely home God heard her cry. " Weeping may endure for a night but her joy came in her morning time.

December 19, 2012 was her morning and God took her home. To the mansion that was not made with hands but it was in the heavens. He took her home cancer free and totally healed from all manner of sickness and disease. He is the Lord thy God that heals. He kept his word and she said she was ready.

Day 2 ______________

Scripture and Notes

Day 3

God does the impossible

"But let him ask in faith, with no doubting, for he who doubts is like a wave of the sea driven and tossed by the wind. For let, not that man suppose that he will receive anything from the Lord; he is a double-minded man, unstable in all his ways ."

— James 1:6-8

Do you believe that God can do the impossible? Not just the "hard," but the truly impossible? Some things just seem to be beyond the realm of our imaginations that we often wonder if God can really accomplish even those things.

A large crowd followed and pressed around him. And a woman was there who had been subject to bleeding for twelve years. She had suffered a great deal under the care of many doctors and had spent all she had, yet instead of getting better she grew worse. When she heard about Jesus, she came up behind him in the crowd and touched his robe, because she thought, "If I just touch his clothes, I will be healed." Immediately her bleeding stopped, and she felt in her body that she was freed from her suffering." (Mark 5:24-35)

We need to understand that when God does not move in our circumstances or when He did not move as fast as we want Him to move, He may be waiting on purpose. Just when we think there is no way out of our situation God steps in on our behalf and performs things that seem so impossible to us.

I remember the time when I had an issue of blood.It lasted twelve long months. It was making me weak, and I was almost to where I would be crawling around the hospital to get help and find that relief. Month after month I would cry out until I was sick. I was hospitalized with the doctors baffled about my treatment. One Sunday I was in church service in Durham when the pastor preached a healing message. I went to the altar and he laid his hands on me and anointed me with oil and the blood stopped immediately. It was 12 months later, and I was weak, but my faith was seeking God for my miracle and it happened Immediately. So, even when it looks impossible to your eye, God is on the scene doing the impossible. He may not come when we want Him to, but He is always on time.

And Jesus said to him, " 'If You can?' All things are possible to him who believes." (Mark 9:23)

Day 3 _____

Scripture and Notes

Day 4

No Thought

"Therefore I say unto you, take no thought for your life, what ye shall eat, or what ye shall drink; nor yet for your body, what ye shall put on. Is not the life more than meat, and the body than raiment?"

— Matthew 6:25

Jesus teaches His followers to help them keep perspective. Some things in life are more important than other things. Your life and body are more important than things, and no one should sacrifice their life and their body simply to get riches or material items, but too many do. Sometimes people work and worry to obtain things and they ruin their mental and physical health, their relationships with God and relationship with others. They show their lack of faith in God's loving desire to give His children all they need. Jesus does not mean that it's wrong to make provisions for our future needs, but we must continue to focus on what is important and that is the Kingdom of God.

I remember there was a time when my husband got out of the military and we had nothing, and I mean nothing. We had two young children and lacked finances, food, and the means to keep a roof over our heads.. God never failed us because we held onto His promises. We took this word and we prayed it and did not waver. We sought the Kingdom and His righteousness-Matthew 6:33 and He did add. He blessed us indeed and increased our territory. God made a way where we saw no way. We took no thought and trusted that He would provide. Not only did He provide, He supplied our every need.

When you think there is no way He has already made a way. God knows our need before we ask Him, and He opens doors we cannot see. Because of the many ambiguities in this world, Jesus knows we need good reasons not to worry. He does not argue against our need to work, save, and prepare for the future, and He enables us to do so. In many places, people lack basic clothing and other everyday necessities. Some cannot afford coats and shoes for the winter.. In other places, people worry about wearing the latest clothing styles for school or work.. How we appear to God in our hearts means more to God than whether we wear the most expensive or stylish clothing, or if we can keep up with the Jones'. But God does not care about all that. He wants our heart. He wants our trust, and He just want us to serve Him fully. He says in Matthew 6:33 But seek first the Kingdom of God and all these things shall be added unto you. Seek means "look for" or go in search for". Once we seek the kingdom of God, or delight ourselves in Him, He will give us all the desires of our heart. Therefore, we have nothing to worry about because He supplies and provides all our need. No worries.

Day 4 _____

Scripture and Notes

Day 5

An Amazing God

And thou shalt remember all the ways which the Lord thy God led thee these forty years in the wilderness, to humble thee, and to prove thee, to know what was in thine heart, whether though would. keep his commandments or no."

— *Deuteronomy 8:2*

It was 2006 and I felt God tugging at my heart to attend a school that was out of my home state of Maryland. God was doing some amazing things in my heart and so I was eager to follow His lead on a new adventure five hours away from home. I had enrolled in school. I had a place lined up. I had a job lined up. I had recently bought a new car. I had just ended a toxic relationship that God clearly did not want me in. I was feeling confident and strong in my faith. I was broke, but I didn't care because I believed that He would take care of me. And He did. But whew! The situation got very scary.

I said my goodbyes, packed up a car full of belongings along with a case of water and Ramen soup, and I ventured to Central Pennsylvania. Within the first month of my stay, the job fell through. I couldn't pay my rent or buy food, and my other bills were already behind. I did all I could, and the rest was up to the Lord. Eventually, he placed me in a job that landed me with a family that took me in. Their huge hearts and love for God resulted in extending a helping hand to me. Now, I wish I could say that I became this faithful, devoted, obedient Christ filled woman after that...but like the Israelites, I soon wandered around grumbling. But God still provided. Through that period in my life, He demonstrated His everlasting kindness and His grace shined down on me. It still does because He is the same yesterday, today, and forever. I can't thank Him enough for how he took care of me.

Tara Matthews

Day 5 _____

Scripture and Notes

Day 6

He Brought Me out

"He has made everything beautiful in its time. He has also set eternity in the human heart, yet no one can fathom what God has done from beginning to end."

— *Ecclesiastes 3:11*

The preacher teaches that a man's activity is ordered in God's timing. Seasons are the most important to farmers; they don't plant during the dry season. There are seasons for all things. Killing and healing during war and peace, maybe even the death penalty for certain crimes. Breaking down and building up, casting stones and gathering stones, tearing and sewing, destroying the old and building new things. Loving and hating, embracing and pushing away, seeking and losing, keeping silent and speaking all involve personal relationships.

How much control do we have over our lives.

God's Spirit stirs my heart to be a woman of divine destiny, but scripture tells us that God has put it in our earthly lives that we are the fulfillment of our dream. God puts dreams in our hearts and writes a destiny over our lives. Our heart and brain should best friends.

When we listen to our heart and trust Him enough to take Him at His word, we will find ourselves on a journey toward the fulfillment of that dream. Unfortunately, the path that takes us to the promise is always wrought with thickets and thorns. Nothing worth having ever comes easy or without opposition.

Storms will come, lions will roar, and our fears will be confronted. God allows the path to be difficult because He intends to be refining us and preparing us for our place of promise. He is intent on extracting from us that which our enemy would love to leverage against us. God loves us too much to promote us before we are ready.

Catherine Walker

Day 6 _____

Scripture and Notes

_____
_____
_____
_____
_____
_____
_____
_____
_____
_____
_____
_____
_____
_____
_____
_____
_____
_____
_____
_____
_____
_____
_____
_____
_____
_____
_____
_____
_____
_____

Day 7

Meaning, Purpose, and Value

There is no entity that has assigned a purpose to life ahead of time. Life just happens. When I tried to give my life meaning, purpose, and value fully my own, I always had a problem not fitting in. I just went with the flow, and life was passing me by. Certainly, I was not unhappy, but I knew I was not complete. There was more to life, more experiences, for me, I just hadn't found it yet. Close! I started out a long time ago, and now here I am finally actively seeking my calling. I am designing and developing my way. I broke free to survey my dream. It takes courage to grow wiser and become. Who am I really supposed to be? I have tried to protect my emotions toward other people when they make me leave my body under certain circumstances. You see my reputation for being very mellow and humble on the rack of feelings. "Have I ever been angry?" I would ask, knowing full well if I am faced with challenges or confrontations with others, I would automatically act nice, without feeling that way. When someone pushes my buttons, it was if I was set to automatically put up my guard with the whole armor of God.

Philippians 2:12-13 Lights in the World

Therefore, my beloved, as you have always obeyed, so now, not only as in my presence but much more in my absence, work out your own salvation with fear and trembling, For it is God who works in you, both to will and to work for his good pleasure.

Catherine Walker

Day 7 _____

Scripture and Notes

_____
_____
_____
_____
_____
_____
_____
_____
_____
_____
_____
_____
_____
_____
_____
_____
_____
_____
_____
_____
_____
_____
_____
_____
_____
_____
_____
_____
_____

Day 8

God Is Preparing You for Great Things

"Now to him who can do far more abundantly than all that we ask or think, according to the power at work within us, and always have the beauty and joy waited upon my goings and comings."

— Ephesians 3:20

Oh, a group of people were going about whatever, so I stopped to see the men and women working on building the biggest project I have ever seen. The building was a school for our babies. I stopped and talked with them as they said, "Good morning! Beautiful day that Lord has made!" I gracefully replied thatyes!! It was indeed a beautiful morning.

Continuing my walk, I started out with God on my mind. As I walked to the end of the road, my legs were hurting and were getting very heavy. I said, "Father, I need you to pick me up along this journey." I believed a devotional journey of life's lessons was upon me. I knew God's promises were true. On my mind, a song appeared. God had a blessing with my name on it.

As I walked my four miles, I knew it was about to happen. Literally making a difference and capturing the goodness of God! As I walked this walk, you see, it made no difference what I was going through. I was going to make it because my God will see me through. I felt great, it was like every bone in my body, and every organ was cleaned out and made new. To the point, I felt him moving all over me. I just want to say I serve a Mighty God. Peace came upon me after I said his name. "Jesus! Mary's baby."

Catherine Walker

Day 8 _____

Scripture and Notes

Day 9

Undeniable Breakthrough of Faith

"Therefore, whosoever heareth these sayings of mine and doeth them, I will liken him unto a wise man, which built his house upon a rock … And everyone that heareth these sayings of mine, and doeth them not, shall be likened unto a foolish man, which built his house upon the sand"

— Matthew 7:24-26

Thank you, Father God, you have given me lots to ponder. This particularly hit home in a mighty way while doing this Journey that I have taken repeatedly. "If your title reveals everything that happens in the story, why bother reading it?" Right.

Of course, some of us live and transform our lives and defeat everything that's blocking our faith by living a life of breakthrough Faith. In your life, we make it clear, when we start walking with breakthrough faith, we need to believe that God is both able and willing. Why is believing both truths and necessary failures in our lives?

When it comes to an undeniable breakthrough of faith. The wise man that hears the voice of God, and acts upon it is abundantly blessed. My theory is when you follow Jesus, you can hear His voice; and when you seek Him, He will speak to you and guide you in all your ways! We've all had some area in our life that we said we are going to change.

Whether it's our relationship, our business, finances, career, health - which we want to take to the next level, but for one reason or another, we just never made it happen. Something we pulled back too soon or didn't follow through. Or maybe we made an excuse or even sabotaged it before we had a chance to start. Whatever the reason, we just couldn't break through with peace of mind.

Catherine Walker

Day 9 _____

Scripture and Notes

Day 10

Infinite Grace

John 3:17 reminds us that "God did not send the Son into the world to condemn the world, but in order that the world might be saved through him" (NRSV). Infinite mercy means incomprehensible mercy. Infinite mercy does not mean condemnation but hope in Christ who came to redeem us from sin and death. God in His infinite mercy will see you through and grant you all your hearts desires.. He will always grant us internal and external journey mercies. God cares for our every need through all hurts. We serve a great God who hears each heartbeat and hears the cry of every broken heart. He is not far away and watching over the clouds, and we can honestly say that he is not limited by our miseries or unaware of our limitations. He knows our frailty. He knows our frustrations, and he also shares in our deepest griefs. I hope I'm understanding my intent, but I see these two qualities—grace and mercy--differently. Since we are followers of Christ, grace and mercy are everlasting. When we are covered by the blood of the lamb, we no longer receive death, but eternal qualities God extends to me or it will be hell for me literally. It reminds me of Romans 6: 1-2: "What shall we say, then? Shall we go on sinning so that grace may increase? By no means! We are those who have died to sin; how can we live in it any longer?" Continuing in sin, if grace will cover it, implies that we think grace is eternal, I think there is a real problem with many confusing God's infinite mercy and grace. It;s only infinite because it comes from and infinite God. But one day it will cease.

Catherine Walker

Day 10 _____

Scripture and Notes

Day 11

If I Regard Iniquity in My Heart

"If I regard iniquity in my heart, the Lord will not hear me."

— *Psalms 66:18*

When my mom was about to transition to her new home, I remember praying the prayer of faith and believing God for healing her, and I know that he did just what was asked of Him. I made sure my heart was cleared and I had forgiven because I wanted to be heard. It wasn't my will, but God's will be done and so was my mother's will. She was ready to move on. It was a sad day, but it was time for her eternal healing. God says in Matthew 7:7 to ask, seek, and knock. If we ask anything in prayer and believe, it shall be done. Prayer is the key component to talking to God. Prayer is our ultimate communication with Him. With prayer and faith, I found out that He can move mountains and heal cancer, and all manner of diseases. I know that prayer changes thing and the mind of God. Then we must look at it this way: If we have sin in our hearts, He will not hear our prayer. So, without a doubt I know God heard my prayer, healed her, and took her home.

Day 11 _____

Scripture and Notes

Day 12

The Fight of Faith

The Lord shall fight for you, and ye shall hold your peace. (Exodus 14:14) There will be things that we will have to encounter, and we will need the Lord to fight for us. We seek God to fight for us in our homes, our marriages, and with our children. The Lord told Moses to "fear ye not, stand still, and see the salvation of the Lord and those Egyptians whom we see then we will not see them again." God is telling us that whatever we may face in our daily walk, He will be with us if we walk in faith and trust Him during the battle. The Lord wants trust to hold our peace and trust by faith that He will bring us through. God has assured His people that He will fight for us if we walk it out by faith (Hebrews 11:1). Without faith, it's impossible to please God. The deliverance of Israel through the Red Sea confirmed God's promises that "He will fight for you. "God assured us that He would definitely fight for us, but we must move forward by faith as He told the Israelites. God fights for His people when they walk in obedience and faith according to His word.

We must put on the whole armor of God and be able to stand against the wiles of the devil (Ephesians 6:10). The Lord will take away from thee all sickness and put none of the evil diseases and He will deliver the enemy before thee: thou shalt smite them. God wants us to be fully equipped in this battle. He has us covered and He will bless us to get through any situation. God desires to heal His people and deliver them out of trouble. He is the Lord thy God who heals (Exodus 15:26).In the book of Exodus God desires to heal his people instead of allowing sickness and diseases to afflict them but it's up to us whether or not we choose to trust God and walk by faith and not by sight, and most of all walk in obedience. So, when hardest of our test and trials come upon us, we should choose to commit our ways unto God instead of accusing Him of neglect and unfaithfulness. We should humbly ask God to show us His ways and lead us into the paths of righteousness for His namesake. We know in the end God will win. The storm may look big but in all actuality it's a small situation. Keep in mind that God will fight for you.

Day 12 _____

Scripture and Notes

Day 13

Spending More Time with God

"Finally, my brethren, be strong in the Lord, and in the power of his might."

— *Ephesians 6:10*

John 15 says that abiding in Him is very important. We cannot do this without Him. We must be connected to his plan and purpose for our lives. Spending time with God may seem hard for some and come easy for others. As we know, when it's time to read His word, sometimes we get tired and distracted by everyday things in our lives. We never find the time to connect with Him until something happens. We need to put on the whole armor of God and be strong in the Lord and in His promises. Unless we abide in Him, we are not connected. Being connected is being in His word and having that relationship with Him, following his commandments and meditating on His word. God has an individual plan for each of us and if we go to Him and abide in His word, we will have that divine connection. Follow the word for yourself and try not to do what someone else does or try to become what someone else is. So finally, my brethren put on the whole armor of God (Ephesians 6). My day includes prayer, intercessory prayer, worship, and praising Him. There are days I fast as well as pray. Be like that tree planted by rivers of water that brings forth fruit in its season. Read and study His word that I consider to be a gift from Him. By reading the bible, studying His word, and fellowshipping with the people of God in bible study, at church, and other things, we become strong in the Lord. Every day my time is different, but by spending time with Him my relationship with Him is strong. Just allow God to direct your paths and lean not unto your own understanding.

Day 13 _____

Scripture and Notes

Day 14

Trusting God When
You Don't Understand

"Though he slays me, yet will I hope in him; I will surely defend my ways to his face."

— Job 13:15

We must learn how to trust God when we don't understand, or when we can't see any way out. We must trust God for our healing and deliverance. Psalm 46:10 says to rest in Him. In other words, to let it go and allow God to move in our lives. Job had so many reasons not to trust God, but he never lost his confidence nor his integrity. Job's children were killed, and so was his livestock, but he never once complained about the situation. Job faced a staggering series of crises and lost a lot. He did not understand what was happening or why God chose him to go through these things. He decided that trusting God would be easier than not. There were times in my life that I may not have understood everything God wanted to show me, but through many heartaches and trials I learned to be still. I learned how to trust God when I had to trust Him after my car accident, when it felt like I lost everything. I felt destroyed and cried more than my fair share of tears. I had to dry up those tears and talk to God. I had to empty out my heart and share my pain. I almost lost my life, but God allowed me to see He was still in charge. My healing was totally in His hands, and in it all I had to trust Him. In being still I had to realize that God is my refuge and strength, a very present help in trouble (Psalm 46:1).

Day 14 _____

Scripture and Notes

Day 15

K HUGS

"Honor your father and your mother, as the LORD your God has commanded you, so that you may live long and that it may go well with you in the land the LORD your God is giving you."

— Deuteronomy 5:15

Faith and death. The moon was out, and it was a beautiful night. I was taking a friend home when I got the call my mother just died alone in her room in California. I had just talked to my mom on April 8th. That was my mother's birthday. Many weeks earlier, I sent all her birthday gifts and Mother's Day gift. I wanted her day to be special, and I wanted her to receive her gifts in time. I am glad she received those gifts in time. I didn't realize that it would be the last time I would see her or give her gifts. I told my mother I love her so much and thanked her. I remember praying for my mother in the hospital. She told me I was the only one of her three that prayed for her. I loved my mother, and I just wish I had more time with her to talk about things like this person I'm talking to, about my career plans, and telling her I received my high school diploma, just so I can hear my mom's voice say she is happy for me and how blessed I am. I will reach all my goals because of Mom, and she will be proud of me. I just wish she was here to share them with me, but I know she is watching over me.

I'm not sure where I where I would be. I thought about suicide or just being alone. Not thoughts about going to New York to Central Park, but just being alone. A sad place to be is alone. Never give in to those thoughts. Instead, listen to God. I am realizing that the best thing I could ever do is thank my mom for all the talks and prayers, and for always talking to God on my behalf. She taught me how to pray for myself and seek God in every situation. She never said I wouldn't have bad days or setbacks, but I just need to keep trusting God. My mom taught me so much. I know she would be proud to know that I am growing in God and that I am walking in the plan and purpose God has for mc.

Kendy Lewis

Day 15 _____

Scripture and Notes

Day 16

The Courage to move on

"Be strong and of good courage, do not fear nor be afraid of them; for the LORD your God, He is the One who goes with you. He will not leave you nor forsake you."

— *Deuteronomy 31:6*

Do you ever feel that you do not have the courage to move on after you have experienced something devastating? I know exactly how this feels because I have been through it. There was nowhere to turn but to God for the courage and strength to endure and to move on. The minute you get down on your knees and pray you can almost immediately feel the weight off your shoulder, strength and faith fully restored.

"For I the Lord thy God will hold thy right hand, saying unto thee, Fear not; I will help thee."

— *Isaiah 41:13*

Remember, the devil is the one who injects us with fear so that we are not able to see the light at the end of that dark and endless tunnel. He does it in such a way that one begins to lose hope, trust, faith, and they believe that this is their outcome. Well, guess what? He tried doing the same to Job and took away everything he ever owned, including his family. He sent Job's friends and even his wife to encourage Job to curse God and die. She wanted Job to give up and walk away. How faithless was that? Job went through it as humans will, his flesh hurt and so did his heart. He was probably grieving the loss of his children, livestock and everything he loved and worked for, but God allowed this to happen. I believe somewhere along the way Job got depressed and bitter, but he never lost his integrity. Job, being a righteous man, never give up. Instead, he prayed not for himself but for his friends.

Daniel and the Hebrew boys had their experiences that required courage; however, at the end of the day, it's not about having courage, but about falling to your knees and asking God to give you courage to overcome things, courage to move on and courage to win. Believe in what you pray for and don't just pray out of habit, but pray because you need to talk to God. Have faith when you ask for victory and courage.

Peter, Jacob and Hezekiah all had the same need for courage, and they prayed. They believed God and watched their situations change. Look at Hezekiah. God added fifteen more years to his life. Jacob wrestled with the angel until he received his blessings. He was broken but didn't let go until God changed his situation. Peter had faith until he looked at his situation and began to sink. We must have the courage to move forward. God can do it! We just need the faith to walk on that water.

Day 16 _____

Scripture and Notes

Day 17

God's Unchanging Hand

"Can anything ever separate us from Christ's love? Does it mean he no longer loves us if we have trouble or calamity, or are persecuted, or hungry, or destitute, or in danger, or threatened with death?"

— Romans 8:35

Jesus tells us that we will have troubles in this world. It's a guarantee. However, He also promises that we have victory through our faith because Jesus Christ has overcome the world. If you are facing hard and uncertain times, you can be encouraged to press on knowing that you are an overcomer!

We must allow God to take charge no matter what the world says, or what the devil tries to do. We must hold on to God's unchanging hand. I have been through the storm and the fire, but I am still here. I am now focusing on what God has planned for me, not what people may say or think. I thank God for changing and letting me listen for His voice. I thank God for how my parents raised me. They showed me Jesus, and taught me that we must love everyone that we meet because it could be an angel that God has sent to you to see how you are going to act.

Love is patient, love is kind, and love is not evil. In my every day walk, I must show the love of God. 1 John 4:7-9 let's us know that God says we must love one another because He is love. That we must show it in our walk everyday with God. My mother always," if you can't say something nice, don't say anything at all." No matter what the world throws at you, remember that God has the final say, so pray for the ones that try to get you to do wrong. I am pushing toward the mark because I am my so much like my mother and no matter what, I am pushing forward to see what is next for me. So, have a high time in the Lord, and give Him the best praise. Tell someone about Jesus because that may be the only way they hear about Him. "You will keep in perfect peace those whose minds are steadfast, because they trust in you." (Isaiah 26:3)

Kimberly Yates Ruperto

Day 17 _____

Scripture and Notes

Day 18

God is Faithful

"There hath no temptation taken you but such as is common to man: but God is faithful, who will not suffer you to be tempted above that ye are able; but will with the temptation also make a way to escape, that ye may be able to bear it."

— 1 Corinthians 10:13

I urge that you hold on unto your faith in Christ and have everlasting hope in him. You cannot deny what is ahead seeing all these natural disasters, which occurs in diverse places in the world, the increase in hunger, poverty and severe crimes on the rise. The signs of times are every where. This is why there's so much more turmoil than ever before. We can only find safety and security in Christ our Lord today.

Trust God's promises because it is where we will find not only safety and security, but everlasting salvation.

We need to fall on our knees and pray unselfishly. Do not pray just for yourself, or for your own family and friends, but also pray for those whom you do not know. Pray for their physical and spiritual healing, and pray for comfort for those who mourn.

I challenge you to pray for ohers today and throughout the week. Now is not the time to be sleeping soundly, but be awake and aware of the upcoming events. This event should not instill fear in you. Instead, have hope that the coming of the Lord is near. It is time we live in a place where there is no more suffering, hunger, dying, hatred or selfishness. I want to be in this place, and I hope to see you there to. Christ has hope that none should perish but all to have eternal life. He has made His move, and now it's your turn to make yours. He has made it all possible for you, but it's up to you to accept it. Salvation is at hand!

Day 18 _____

Scripture and Notes

Day 19

Divine Connection

"I am the true vine, and My Father is the vinedresser. Every branch in Me that does not bear fruit He takes away; and every branch that bears fruit He prunes, that it may bear more fruit."

— *John 15:1-2*

You are expected to bear fruit regardless of your circumstances. Fruitfulness requires action. If you want something to happen then you need to act. You cannot expect to see fruit if you do not sow or plant. Fruitfulness does not appear magically. You reap what you sow. You receive what you put in. Jesus is the vine and we are the branches (John 15). He instructs that if we remain in Him and His words remain in us, that is, if we are deeply connected to Him and whatever He says lives in our hearts, whatever we ask for we shall receive. The reality is that branches receive nutrients from the vine. The branch survives based on what it receives from the vine. In other words, the kind of fruitfulness we seek can only be found when we are connected to Christ. As the branch, is your connection to Christ the Vine secure enough to produce fruit? Is there anything blocking you from receiving the nutrients from Christ in order to be fruitful? God did not create us to be one-time fruit bearers. The Scripture teaches us that "every branch that continues to bear fruit, He [continually] prunes, so that it will bear more fruit [even richer and finer fruit]" (John 15:1-2). You are God's investment. He wants you to bear fruit and that is why He has cut off dead things around you. When you bear fruit, He helps you to continue to bear more fruit. He just wants us to abide in Him. By remaining attached to Him, we will never be without fruit. He continually prunes us by removing things from our lives that diverts or hinders the vital life flow of Christ in us. His fruit is the quality of Christian character that brings Him glory. So, we are either going to be fruitful or fruitless.

Day 19 _____

Scripture and Notes

Day 20

No Greater Love

"Nor height, nor depth, nor any other creature, shall be able to separate us from the love of God, which is in Christ Jesus our Lord."

— Roman 8:39

When we hear the word love, what comes to mind? According to the Webster Dictionary, love is "an intense feeling of deep affection." When you love someone, it is hard to see them go through a series of painful events, yet God, sent his only begotten son to be crucified on Calvary, just because he possesses such love for us. Romans 5:8 "But God commended his love toward us, in that, while we were yet sinners, Christ died for us." If we fully comprehend the meaning of true love, then we will understand what the Father has done for us. Even when we do understand, we often take it for granted.

Love is the essence of gospel and living in the light of His love is essential if we are to be transformed into the image of the One who saved us. It is critical for us to think about, come to know and understand the love of God, because only His love will grant us the joy that strengthens our hearts, the courage that reassures us to fight against sin, and the assurance of His care for us. As we come to know His love, we come to know who our God really is and how He redeems us, freeing us from sin's curse and our own guilt and shame.

The Father realized that the only way we could have victory over sin is to have His only Son crucified. There is no greater love for us than the love of Christ.

Everyday, let us take some time to give thanks for the fact that we now have victory over sin through Christ our Lord. Christ has not withheld anything from us. He said, "ask it shall be given and knock, and the door shall be open for us." He has given it all to us and all we need to do is to receive it with a clean and open heart.

Please share the love of God with someone today. It inspires, it forgives, and it overcomes all.

Day 20 _____

Scripture and Notes

_____
_____
_____
_____
_____
_____
_____
_____
_____
_____
_____
_____
_____
_____
_____
_____
_____
_____
_____
_____
_____
_____
_____
_____
_____
_____
_____
_____
_____
_____
_____
_____
_____

Day 21

Working for My Good

"And we know that all things work together for good to them that love God, to them who are the called according to his purpose."

— *Romans 8:28*

There are many things in our lives that make us happy. To some, money is one of those things. The main things in my life that make me happy are my marriage, my children, my health, my life and especially the Lord. Some people find happiness in things, materialistic things. These are the things that God said will soon fade away. For some, happiness revolves around their friends, their romantic relationships, their jobs, even sports. As for me for me, there are times when I find happiness in just a good old piece of candy. Yes, I seem to find enjoyment there, but this is just one of my wordly pleasures. There are times I go to the store and get a Milky Way or a Twix bar and find peace eating that candy. But one thing is for sure, it's not that perfect peace and it's just a temporary joy. I enjoy eating it bite after bite, and its good until the end, then it's all gone. A temporary fix.

There are many things in life that can bring happiness, but I find the most happiness in God. We all experience personal issues that turn our world upside down. We don't know which way to turn. We may cry, scream and shout. Depression may come upon some. Psalms 30:5 says, "weeping may endure for a night, but joy comes in the morning." Our morning can be at any time. This scripture allows us to see that no matter what happens in our life, God will bring us through it. James 1:3 says to "count it all joy." One might wonder how they can count this all joy when cancer hit their family. How can we count it all joy when death comes to our door? In other words, we must trust in God because "all things work together for the good of those who love the Lord." (Romans 8:28) We must trust God no matter what it looks like. Though weeping may endure for a night, just remember that God will always dry our tears.

The more we learn about what God expects of us, the greater the victory we will live in this present world.

For now, things may be rough, but when we come to Him in prayer and with faith even small as a mustard seed, we see change. It is such an honor to serve the Almighty God.

Day 21 _____

Scripture and Notes

Day 22

Be transformed

"Therefore, if any man be in Christ, he is a new creature: old things are died; behold, all things are become new."

— *2 Corinthians 5:17*

It is quite amazing that when someone is fully converted in Christ you can see the almost instant changes in appearance, speech, demeanor and so on. I am sure that each person reading this has had this blessed experience of transformation, be it great or small. I speak to you today about the power of prayer and faith.

Prayer is the way of communicating with God, and faith is the assurance that whatever you ask, He will answer. Therefore, you can see how these two go hand-in-hand. Hebrews 11:6 - And without faith it is impossible to please Him, for he who comes to God must believe that He is and that He is a rewarder of those who seek Him. James 5:14 - 15 - Is anyone among you sick? Then he must call for the elders of the church and they are to pray over him, anointing him with oil in the name of the Lord; and the prayer offered in faith will restore the one who is sick, and the Lord will raise him up, and if he has committed sins, they will be forgiven him.

Through prayer and with faith we have seen or read of many transformations. Consider Job, Daniel, the three Hebrew boys, the woman at the well, the woman with the infirmity, and many more. Their story speaks about their great conversions and transformations because they believed faithfully. Today, you can have your own personal deliverance and be transformed as well. What it takes to be transformed is free and priceless, but the value it lays on you is high, for you are bought and highly favored by Jesus Christ. Come to the foot of the cross today. Kneel before His presence and communicate to him passionately, in faith, and you are bound to see a change, a new thing before your eyes. Once you have been touched by Jesus Christ, you can never be the same. Today, I pray that you pursue God and see changes in the family, marriage, finance, work, school and of course your relationship, not just with others, but with the Heavenly Father.

Day 22 _____

Scripture and Notes

Day 23

Do you feel blessed today?

"Count it all joy, my brothers, when you meet trials of various kinds, for you know that the testing of your faith produces steadfastness. And let steadfastness have its full effect, that you may be perfect and complete, lacking in nothing."

— James 1:2

When you wander upon God's wonderful work and know that you are the highest of His creation, you feel blessed. He is not just the author of life, but also the leader of it. How does the bird know to chirp in the morning? How does the rooster know the crow at dawn? Because He said "let everything that have breath praise the Lord" (Psalms 100). He gave them life and the strength to fly and the breath to make that joyful noise each day. (John 12 :7 -12) But ask the animals, and they will teach you, or the birds in the sky, and they will tell you; or speak to the earth, and it will teach you, or let the fish in the sea inform you. Which of all these does not know that the hand of the LORD has done this? In his hand is the life of every creature and the breath of all mankind.

Daily, as I look out my window, I watch squirrels walking all over the yard, looking for food and carrying off those acorns. They swiftly climb the trees and go home. God supplies and provides for them.

God has everything in his control so believe that once you have faith, he will make a way to solve every issue and dry every tear. When you look at your life today and see where are now from where you were before, you ought to be grateful that thedevastating moments in your life did not last forever. Get down on your knees thank Him. Believe that He has solved them once and that He will do it once again.

God promised He would supply and provide, and He does so daily. We must continue to walk by faith and not by sight. We must trust Him each day with our lives and know that He will never leave us nor forsake us, and that we are to be strong and very courageous.

Day 23 _____

Scripture and Notes

Day 24

Give Thanks

"For of him, and through him, and to him, are all things: to who be glory forever. Amen."

— *Romans 11:36*

Aren't you grateful for being alive and well this morning? Give thanks to God; give Him glory. Everything we do we must do it to the glory of God. What does it mean to give glory? How can one give glory to God? Some may be thinking, if God has all the glory, how we can give him glory?

"The word glory as related to God in the Old Testament bears with it the idea of greatness of splendor." He is the Almighty, the Lords and lords, he Kings and kings, and the only true God.

In the New Testament, the word translated "glory" means "dignity, honor, praise, and worship." Therefore,, we find that glorifying God means to acknowledge His greatness and to give Him honor by praising and worshiping Him, primarily because He, and He alone, deserves to be praised, honored and worshipped. God's glory is the essence of His nature, and we give glory to Him by recognizing that essence.

We give glory in everything that we do. Whatever we eat, drink, or say should all be to the glory of God.

Other ways to give God glory is through prayers, praises, singing, and being thankful for all things which He made possible for you. Sister, you cannot want the gifts but not the Giver of the gifts. God is so merciful, and He does not force us to worship Him, but we should at least be thankful and acknowledge Him. You cannot try to be holy but not accept the One who is pure in holiness. How would you feel if someone keeps taking from you and has nothing to give you in return, not even their gratitude?

Day 24 _____

Scripture and Notes

Day 25

Trusting God in your hardest time

"As the deer pants for streams of water, so my soul pants for you, my God."

— *Psalm 42:1*

Have you ever been through a strong depression? Or perhaps just felt blue because it was snowing outside and you felt closed in? It's the emotional let down you may feel when it seems like the holidays didn't work out, or maybe the grief is so real that you can't shake it. We can feel overwhelmed when life gets crazy and circumstances seem to completely take over our lives. When I read this psalm, it let me see that I wasn't the only one going through these kind of hard times, that and there may be others whose souls are panting after God as well. We need to remember that God's presence can give us the encouragement that we need. He will be there for us in our toughest moments and help us to rise above our circumstances.

Difficult times are real, and as we look around us the earth is filled with hard and unexpectant twists. Depression is real, too, and sometimes awful. It's when the weight of life looks like a giant.It overwhelms and presses hard upon us. We may get stunned now, but then we think about the goodness of Jesus and all He has done for us, and that weight lifts off of us. Even the moments we may fall into depression, we should remember that God is good and that we can overcome with His help. Trust God and know He will bring you out.

When hard times arrive in our lives, we do have a choice. We can choose to pray, worship, encourage others, or find help to get us through. (Psalms 46:1)- God is our refuge and strength, a very present help in trouble. Just remember that we can trust Him to bring us through in everything we may face. He is the author and finisher of our faith. He is our shepherd and we have no need (Psalms 23:1). Just remember that God never gives up on his promises, including the promise that He will never leave us nor forsake us. Just trust Him in it all. By faith He will work it out.

Day 25 _____

Scripture and Notes

_____
_____
_____
_____
_____
_____
_____
_____
_____
_____
_____
_____
_____
_____
_____
_____
_____
_____
_____
_____
_____
_____
_____
_____
_____
_____
_____
_____
_____
_____
_____
_____
_____

Day 26

Shelter of the Almighty

"Whoever dwells in the shelter of the Highest will rest in the shadow of the Almighty. I will say that the Lord is my refuge and my fortress: my God; in him will I trust."

— Psalm 91:1

This psalm expresses the security that we will have if we trust God. It assures us that God will be our refuge, and we just need to seek His protection when we go through spiritual and physical danger. He will take us through it. The more we abide in Him and His word, and if we make Him our life and dwelling place, the more we will be at peace and the greater our deliverance will be when we are in danger. Nothing can happen if we are a faithful servant. He will continue to lift us up in our time of trouble because "He is our refuge and strength a very present help in trouble" (Psalms 46:1). God commissions angels to watch over His faithful believers and those who continually dwell in His presence. They lift us when we are in trouble and support us as we face our spiritual enemies. Ephesians 6:10 Finally, be strong in the Lord and in His mighty power. Sometimes we may go through spiritual bareness, but God is there during that time of insecurity and instability. He gives us the power to face the uncertainties and adversities of life. God is faithful and therefore we must remember He that dwelleth in the secret place of the Highest shall abide under the shadow of the almighty -Psalms 91:1 He is our shelter!

Day 26 _____

Scripture and Notes

_____

_____

_____

_____

_____

_____

_____

_____

_____

_____

_____

_____

_____

_____

_____

_____

_____

_____

_____

_____

_____

_____

_____

_____

_____

_____

_____

_____

_____

Day 27

In Everything Give Thanks

"Give thanks in all circumstances; for this is God's will for you in Christ Jesus."

— *1 Thessalonians 5:18*

There are so many things to be thankful for, and we need to give thanks in all things. If we start making a list of the things we are thankful for, we may appreciate the big and small things in life. There are many things that we take for granted because we have such an abundance of them. There are people in countries like Uganda, and in many other countries, who are lacking. They would feel wealthy if they had all the things we throw away! Some of these countries need food, clothing, and clean water. We have many means of transportation and ways to get around, but they walk, sometimes with no shoes, and must walk everywhere they go. When my children waste food or think they need the most expensive things to wear, I tell them to consider the children without. In all things they need to be thankful. In the days of my youth, our parents would provide us with the food and clothing we needed. These things were not the fanciest ones or the most expensive types of clothing, but our needs were met. We had to eat all our food and couldn't waste any. If we didn't like something, we still had to eat it. We were thankful for our needs being met. My God shall supply all my needs (Philippians 4:19). We should not just give God praise when things are going great. But give Him thanks always. Give thanks in everything: for this is the will of God in Christ Jesus concerning you (I Thessalonians 5:18).

Day 27 _____

Scripture and Notes

Day 28

Spending More Time with God

"Finally, my brethren, be strong in the Lord, and in the power of his might."

— Ephesians 6:10

Do you struggle to spend more time with God each day? Is it a constant battle between spending time with Him and distracting yourself with social media? Are you on the phone talking to everyone else but can't find time to pray? Does it feel like you're in one corner of the ring with the Holy Spirit is in the other corner, and you are in a real knock-down-drag-out?

Spending time with God may seem hard for some and come easy for others. When it's time to read His Word, we sometimes get tired or distracted by everyday things in our lives. Maybe you want to read the Bible more but find yourself putting it off to enjoy more "fun" reading.

We never find the time until something happens. We need to define our distractions. What hinders us from reading God's Word? Is it that we want to get on social media as soon as we wake up ? Do we want to call a friend before we get our Bible and prayer time in? What has taken you away from spending time with God first thing in the morning? What keeps you from praying throughout the day. God doesn't just want a short and quick prayer. He desires that intimate time with us through prayer and His Word. That is how we get to know Him personally.

Unless we abide in Him, we are not connected. Being connected is being in His Word and having a close, personal relationship with Him, following His commandments and meditating on His word. God has an individual plan for each of us, and if we go to Him and abide in His Word, we will have that divine connection.

- Establish a regular place and time
- Minimize Distractions
- Start with prayer
- Meditate
- Journal

By reading the Bible and meditating on His word, and by fellowshipping with the people of God in Bible study, at church, and other social events, we become strong in the Lord. Every day my time is different, and by spending time with Him my relationship in Him is strong. Just allow God to direct your path and lean not unto your own understanding.

Day 28 _____

Scripture and Notes

Day 29

Faith Is Trusting God in Everything.

"For it is by grace you have been saved, through faith—and this is not from yourselves, it is the gift of God—not by works, so that no one can boast."

— *Ephesians 2:8-9*

Trusting God in all circumstances enables the believer to persevere and remain steadfast in His word. We must trust God to help us through every situation . We must trust God for healing when we are sick (Isaiah 53:5). We must trust Him for finances.. Faith is when we take God's Word and pray it over our situation and believe for the outcome. Faith without works is dead. When doing counseling and any type of ministry, I certainly need faith that will move mountains. When I travel from conference-to-conference or to my workshops, I need mountain-moving faith for a great outcome. When setting up the conferences and workshops, I need faith to go out to speak to the ladies. I have faith that God will use my gift to help transform lives. So, that "now faith" that is spoken about in Hebrews 11:1 "is the substance of things hoped for and the evidence that we do not see." We know without a doubt that God will work something out in our lives. Having that "now faith" means that we will trust that God is in every situation and in all our circumstances. This kind of faith leads to righteousness and seeks God and believes Him for everything. This faith is obedient to His commands and endures persecution. It has confidence in God's Word and refuses to have any pleasure in sin. Faith is that steadfast trust in God and that His ways are correct. God says that His Word will not come back empty and it will accomplish everything that He said it would. Trusting God in everything means that we will have no doubt that He can perform just what He says He can do. Habakkuk 2:4 says, "the just shall live by faith."

Day 29 _____

Scripture and Notes

Day 30

A New Thing

God says, "Behold I will do a new thing now and it will spring forth, shall ye not know it? I will make a water in the wilderness and rivers in the desert" (Isaiah 43: 19). Spring forth- (to leap out- rush out, arise and to come into existence) It's going to leap out and I will see that new thing come to pass. There were times I felt as if I was in the wilderness and didn't know whether God heard my prayers or not. I felt spiritually dry and it was as if my prayers weren't being heard and it was even difficult to enjoy the Lord. It was a spiritual depression and felt as if there was no way out. But God said He would give me that water in the wilderness and that it would come forth. He said that He would do a brand-new thing and take me to a land was new to me. The transition was hard, and I had to get through it, but He provided and supplied.

My husband and I moved into a smaller place in Wilson, NC. Transitioning was hard, and letting go was, too. It ended up being the perfect size for the both of us. Our empty nest years had given my husband and me time to reconnect and discover things we can pursue together. God took the emptiness I felt and gave me fullness. It opened new doors and allowed us to be even closer in our marital relationship and with God. If you are struggling, try to look at your empty nest as an opportunity for something new in your life. Know that God has a plan and purpose for your life. God brought us to a new land, in a new season in our lives, to do new things. Old things died and behold there will be new things. Since we have been here, God has shown himself strong, and amazing things have happened. We are greatly satisfied. Isaiah 43:19- God says He would make a way in the wilderness and for us to let go of the past and move forward. He continues to work in us every day. He gives us a fresh anointing. God said that He would give us new mercies each day (Lamentations 3:22-24). God renews His grace in every situation we face. Doing a new thing means we move to a new level of freedom that we have never known before.

Day 30 _____

Scripture and Notes

Day 31

Are you faithing it?

"For by grace are ye saved through faith; and that not of yourselves: it is the gift of God."

— Ephesians 2:8

"Yea, a man may say, thou hast faith, and I have works: show me thy faith without thy works, and I will show thee my faith by my works."

—James 2:18

I know that faithing it isn't exactly a word in the dictionary, but are you faithing it? The bible speaks of the "now faith." The kind of faith that can move mountains. The bible teaches us about the kind of faith that healed a lady that had an issue of blood for twelve long years and all it took was one touch of the hem of the Master's garment. In Luke chapter 13 it tells about another lady who was bent over for 18 long years. They called it an infirmity. She struggled with this for a long time. I call her The woman that was bent out of Shape. She was faithing it. She heard that there was a man that could heal anybody. She decided to see it his way. Jesus spoke to her situation, touched her heart, and ministered to that little girl inside of her. He said, "woman thou art loosed" and she was straightened up immediately. It was by her faith. So, you see, if she didn't believe and instead doubted Jesus, she would still be bent out of shape. Then, Jesus met a man at the pool who couldn't walk and had been bedridden for 38 years. By faith and trusting Jesus to just speak to his situation and "take up thy bed and walk," he did exactly that. Faith without works is dead. We must trust God at his word. By faith I was healed from my issues and from many situations in my life. By faith God healed my mind after a miscarriage. I was faithing it and still do in my everyday life. This was a saying that the older ladies in the church used to say: Prayer is the key and faith unlocks the door. When we pray, we must believe, we must stand strong on His Word and waver not. Prayer is a powerful tool, and by praying and believing we are exercising our faith, and by faith we know that God hears. This is how we invite God to get involved in our situations. We communicate to Him our needs and He supplies them by faith and through prayer. After we have prayed , we must then walk by faith and begin speaking it into the atmosphere and doubt not. We must act as if we already got our answer. I remember when I asked God to heal my body after having that issue and I knew that only He could heal me. By faith I prayed and trusted Him to remove that sickness and allow me to be free. I believed, and it came to pass. Trusting in and believing God for the things we cannot see but know that God is able to bring it to pass, by faith we are made whole.

Day 31 _____

Scripture and Notes

_____
_____
_____
_____
_____
_____
_____
_____
_____
_____
_____
_____
_____
_____
_____
_____
_____
_____
_____
_____
_____
_____
_____
_____
_____
_____
_____
_____
_____
_____

Day 32

Mountain-Moving Faith

"Have faith in God," Jesus answered. "Truly I tell you, if anyone says to this mountain, 'Go, throw yourself into the sea,' and does not doubt in their heart but believes that what they say will happen, it will be done for them."

— Mark 11:22-24

Faith is the assurance of things hoped for, the evidence of things not seen. We can't see it, but we know that God will do it. Faith is also trusting in God in all our circumstances, which enables us as a believer, and all we need to do is to stay loyal to God and His Word at all times.

Believe and ye shall receive. God himself imparts faith into the believer's heart. Sometimes our desires are granted immediately and other times they are not. But God gives us the faith to let us know that our prayers have been answered and that His forgiveness has been granted. All we need to do is to trust God and believe Him and take Him at his word. He told us to speak to it. Speak to that mountain. Tell that situation to move and then let it go.

I can remember asking God to move on my behalf. The doctor thought I had thyroid cancer. I told him with conviction that I was healed and stood on God's word. I began to speak to that situation and trusted God for the outcome. After surgery was over and the results were released, the doctor said the tumor was benign. I praised God for the outcome because He does not lie (Numbers 23:19-20). His word says He will heal and deliver and set us free. God said without faith it's impossible to please Him and He is a rewarder of they that seek Him diligently (Hebrews 11:6). Seek Him earnestly and faithfully and your blessings will come exceedingly and abundantly.

This passage of scripture also makes it plain to us that if we pray and don't forgive, He will not forgive us of our trespasses and therefore our prayers will be hindered. We cannot hold any animosity or bitterness in our hearts if we expect to hear from God. We must forgive and ask God to create in us a clean heart and renew the right spirit within us (Psalm 51:10).

Day 32 _____

Scripture and Notes

_____

_____

_____

_____

_____

_____

_____

_____

_____

_____

_____

_____

_____

_____

_____

_____

_____

_____

_____

_____

_____

_____

_____

_____

_____

_____

_____

_____

_____

Day 33

Joy Comes in the Morning

"Weeping may endure for a night, but joy comes in the morning."

— Psalm 30:5

In our lives we face disappointments, sadness, and stress. We can't escape them. That is a part of life. We can't avoid all of life's tests, trials, and seasons. We must endure and embrace the storms in life. Psalm 30:5 says that weeping may endure for a night, but joy comes in the morning. We must deal with the heartaches, sadness, grief, and other emotions in our lives, but God promised us that if we just hold on our morning is coming. We must learn how to let the spirit of joy back into our lives at the time of sadness and not allow guilt to come in and make us feel heavy about feeling enjoyment after our disappointments. The Word of God says that He will keep us in perfect peace if we keep our mind on Him and if we trust Him. He will give us the joy needed in the middle of our situation. But we must stay in touch with our emotions and realize that God is a healer and that trouble doesn't last forever. We must trust that God can bring us through any situation.

There have been times that I have been sad because my mom is no longer here, and I have cried without end. I have had dreams about her, and the pain seemed to have no end. But God promised me peace during my situation and patience as I went through it. He promised me that everything would be alright. I can say that weeping has endured for a night, but joy came during my mo(u)rning. I can now rejoice and see that everything has a season and God has a purpose for everything under the sun. God knew what was best for my mother and I do not question that, despite the pain it left us with and the hurt that we had to endure. I was sad of course, and my emotions may have been a little out of control, but I can now rejoice in the pain and suffering, and I know that my morning has come. I can see the joy in it all. I may have wept and sometimes still do,, but I know the true meaning of joy because God has shown me that he has a plan and purpose for it all. I have joy in my mo(u)rning.

Day 33 _____

Scripture and Notes

Day 34

Trust Him to Fight For You

"The Lord shall fight for you, and ye shall hold your peace."

— Exodus 14:14

There will be battles you encounter that you will need the Lord to fight for you. We seek God to fight for us in our homes, our marriages, and with our children. God fighting our battles means we do not have to be in anguish, be anxious, or be discouraged when bad things happen. When it seems a situation is hopeless or that the matter at hand is too overwhelming, we may be tempted to doubt God, but if you continue to trust Him, He will see you through.

The Lord told Moses to "fear ye not, stand still, and see the salvation of the Lord and those Egyptians whom we see then we will not see them again." God is telling us that whatever we may face in our daily walk, He will be with us if we walk in faith and trust Him during the battle. The Lord wants us to hold our peace and trust Him by faith that He will bring us through. God has assured His people that He will fight for us if we walk out by faith (Hebrews 11:1). God will fight for us. Without faith, it's impossible to please God. The deliverance of Israel through the Red Sea confirmed God's promise that "He will fight for you" (Ephesians 6:10). We must put on the whole armor of God and be able to stand against the wiles of the devil. He wants us to be fully equipped in this battle. The Lord will take away from thee all sickness and put none of the evil diseases and He will deliver the enemy before thee: thou shalt smite them. God has us covered and he will bless us to get through any situation.

The weapons of our warfare are not carnal but mighty through God to the pulling down of strong holds (2 Corinthians 10:4).

Day 34 _____

Scripture and Notes

Day 35

My Secret Place

"He that dwelleth in the secret place of the highest shall abide under the shadow of the Almighty."

— *Psalm 91:1*

My secret place is in my heart. I go there to find myself, in this locked away place where it's just me and God. I created and copyrighted a space just for me. God is a great listener. He guides me in the way I need to go. Every person has a need for some secrecy in their lives, occasionally. When I was a child, I had a special secret place where I went to when I needed to have some privacy, and it had always been my heart. In the summer when we went to the beach with family, I was always alone with my dreams. My heart has always been a place where I could escape from the everyday mess of adults and back-biting people. I remember being home on my front porch, where we had this place with a lush lawn and lots of flowers and trees. The grass bloomed bright green and was perfectly cut. There was a couple of fountains and many birds were resting on the branches in the shadow of the trees. Some of them chirped constantly in anticipation of getting a reply. It was wonderful and I enjoyed the peaceful atmosphere to the fullest. I would often visit my secret place while sitting out there on the porch.

God has been working on me lately. I've been so busy trying to be the best I can be. The busier I become, the more I push God onto the back burner. I know many of you can relate: the more things we must juggle, the easier it becomes to make God less of a priority. As I reflect to those weeks, it breaks my heart to think of how patient and oh so merciful Christ was as I ran my life without Him, only giving Him the last bit of my day. You know, those days when you're burnt-out and extremely exhausted from the day's activities, so you just say a quick 1-minute lifeless prayer that your heart isn't even into, all while you're falling asleep. Ring any bells?

Catherine Walker

Day 35 _____

Scripture and Notes

Day 36

Wait on the Lord

"I waited patiently for the LORD; he turned to me and heard my cry. He lifted me out of the slimy pit, out of the mud and mire; he set my feet on a rock and gave me a firm place to stand. He put a new song in my mouth, a hymn of praise to our God. Many will see and fear the LORD and put their trust in him."

— Psalms 40:1:3

We must wait on God's plans for our lives to develop. In our waiting, we must wait patiently with expectancy. I continue to wait. There may be times when we may ask for something and it's not time for us to have it. There was a time I wanted this car so badly and through all my impatience God gave it to me. I got it with much suffering because if I had waited the interest rate may not have been so high and my payments may have been lower. Had I been patient, I would not have got behind on those payments, causing it to be taken away. I got it back and suffered through until it was paid for. While we wait, we must be patient; we must wait quietly (Psalms 62:1) and do it without complaining. We must wait and trust God (Proverbs 3:5-6). God sees what is in front of us and what is behind us. He knows everything about us and more.

How do you wait?

- Do you wait for Him patiently?
- Do you wait murmuring and complaining?
- Do you wait anxiously?
- Do you wait questioning everything?

We should wait expectantly (Psalms 27:13). Wait until we have God's permission for certain decisions and His guidance and direction. Sometimes it takes some courage to wait on Him. God knows what is best for us. He may say wait longer because we may not be ready for it. There are some things He may say "no" to because it would cause us to sin. God is always in the process of teaching us how to trust in Him and teaching us to wait. Isaiah 40:31- When we wait our strength is renewed, and maybe then He will release that promise to us.

Day 36 _____

Scripture and Notes

Day 37

Choose Happiness

"This is the day the Lord has made; let us rejoice and be glad in it."

— Psalm 118:24

There will be challenges that you must face and circumstances that may weigh you down, but how you choose to respond is up to you. It's up to you how you live your life. This is the day that the Lord has made, and we will rejoice. In other words, no matter what the day brings, no matter what what it may look like, the choice is ours how we take this day on. It is dependent on your choice. If you have the right mind set, you can choose to be happy and rejoice as you are going through challenges, or you can choose to take it another way and create a different type of day that is not so good. Give yourself permission to be happy each day.

Whatever today holds, I will rejoice because God made this day. He called me into this day, He ordained this day that I would walk in it and be glad. He already knew what this day would hold for me, and He will be with me every second of this day. It's my choice how I will go through this day and every day. God made it and He knew each detail of this day. I will then choose to be happy in it because no matter what comes or goes I know He will be there.

In Psalm 118, the author is writing about incredible adversity. It's not written when times are good, but when times are hard. Situations were changing. The Psalmist cried out to God in anguish, he was surrounded by the enemy. He was pushed back and about to fall. Yet, right during huge scuffles, this chapter begins and ends with the same verse, of giving thanks and praise unto God.

Give thanks to the Lord, for he is good, his love endures forever

Day 37 _____

Scripture and Notes

Day 38

Become Someone Else's Miracle

"We are therefore Christ's ambassadors, as though God were making his appeal through us. We implore you on Christ's behalf: Be reconciled to God."

— 2 Corinthians 5:20

Every day, we are praying for someone's miracle. It could be marriage, cancer, diabetes or some other illness, but someone we know needs a miracle. We trust God and take Him at His word. Everywhere we go there are people in need of a miracle. They may be smiling on the outside but hurting on the inside. Many are quietly hurting and choose not to share with anyone. Everyone has a ministry, a calling or purpose. It does not have to be in the pulpit, but God is counting on each one of us to reach out to those who are hurting or in need and bring His healing everywhere we go.

Our job is not to judge. Instead, God wants us to speak life to those who are down and going through pain. Too often people do not know how to reach out for help. But pray and be prepared to reach out to someone who is hurting or needing guidance. Too often we focus on our own problems, goals, dreams and hopes for a miracle that we don't have time for someone else's. When we become someone's miracle, there is healing in your land and healing in your situation.

The woman with the issue of blood knew she needed help after 12 long years of suffering and she decided to push her way through the crowd. She knew she shouldn't be there, but she was tired, hopeless and she had heard Jesus was passing by and so by faith she pressed through the crowd for her miracle. God felt her touch and she was delivered immediately.

We must be serious about pushing our way through our situations and allowing God to see our faith. He knows what we need before we ask, but we need to act like the woman who knew that one touch was all it would take. She heard a word and moved out on faith. Faith comes by hearing and without it we cannot please God. It was all in the pressing.

Day 38 _____

Scripture and Notes

Day 39

The Meaning of Transformation

"Do not conform to the pattern of this world but be transformed by the renewing of your mind. Then you will be able to test and approve what God's will is-his good, pleasing and perfect will."

— Romans 12:2

God's priority for us is transformation. He wants to change us from the inside out. He always takes us through transformation before He transforms our situation or circumstances. When God lead the children out of Egypt, he knew that they would need to change their mindset in order to enter the Promised Land. Because of their murmuring and complaining, that eleven-day journey took them forty years. Their minds needed to be transformed and renewed, and they needed to trust God in the process. We all have that wilderness experience we must endure, and most of all we must trust God in that season. In our experiences and transformation, we must know that God is able to bring us through.

He perfects everything that concerns us. If we are stressed out all the time, something will have to change for the stress to be relieved. It won't go away if we keep doing the same things repeatedly. If you want different results, you must change what you are doing. Take some bold steps of faith and change anything in your life that God leads you to transform. If what you are doing is not bearing fruit, then change it. If you aren't getting enough rest, then make a change. God's word in 2 Kings 4:8 states," it is well" and it shall be well. Just make that change. You may be afraid of making changes in life, but it is also possible that if you can find the courage to make that change, others around you will also do it . Don't be afraid, but do it fearlessly. If you don't make those changes and if you don't act on it, you will still be complaining. It is time to make a change in your life. Don't waste your time resisting change. God will use it to mold us and make us into our New. When we make changes, it keeps life fresh and exciting- so welcome change with faith and trust in God, because He will pull you through every situation by faith.

Deuteronomy 8:2 says Remember how the LORD your God led you all the way in the wilderness these forty years, to humble and test you in order to know what was in your heart, whether or not you would keep his commands or not. If we embrace the wilderness by faith and trust God. It will be a place where we are free from bondage to our fears, insecurities, and disappointments. It will be a place we learn to live wholeheartedly and to fully embrace the plans and purposes that God has for us. Be transformed by renewing your mind.

Day 39 _____

Scripture and Notes

_____

_____

_____

_____

_____

_____

_____

_____

_____

_____

_____

_____

_____

_____

_____

_____

_____

_____

_____

_____

_____

_____

_____

_____

_____

_____

_____

_____

_____

_____

_____

_____

_____

_____

_____

_____

Day 40

Pray or Worry, but You Can't Do Both

"Trust in the lord with all thine heart and lean not unto thine own understanding."

— *Proverbs 3:5*

Trusting God even when you don't understand. That was the situation Sarah and Abraham were put in. Abraham must have thought that they were too old, and it may have seemed impossible, but Abraham trusted God in his situation. Sarah was looking through her natural eyes and thought that giving birth would be impossible at her age. She even went as far as laughing.

In my own walk, giving birth to my dreams at times seemed very impossible, and I often felt that I was too old to accomplish my dream or reach any goals that I had set for myself. Well, God allowed me to read and see that if Sarah could give birth to a baby at her age, then I can bring life to my goals. I began to walk into my destiny, still working on the promises of God. Like Sarah, I felt like giving up on my dream, at times because I was worried about the situation instead of praying. I had to trust God in it all and I went on and got my college degrees. I am thankful that I trusted God in it all. Yes, I laughed and I cried, but I went through and made it. I was pushed into my destiny.

Sarah had a plan of her own and it didn't work out. Why? Because it wasn't God's plan for her life. Sometimes we step in the way and mess it all up, and our waiting is longer than before. God's ways are not our ways and his thoughts aren't ours (Isaiah 55:8). His thoughts and ways are not that of a carnal person. But our minds can be transformed by trusting in His promises and abiding in His Word. Worry is not in His plan for us because worry is not of God. It is prayer that moves mountains, not worrying.

Trust God with all your heart and lean not unto your own understanding. Because there is a way that seems right unto man and appears straight but at the end is death. If you don't know the Word of God, you will not know the will of God. Trust, pray, but do not worry.

Day 40 _____

Scripture and Notes

_____

_____

_____

_____

_____

_____

_____

_____

_____

_____

_____

_____

_____

_____

_____

_____

_____

_____

_____

_____

_____

_____

_____

_____

_____

_____

_____

_____

_____

_____

_____

_____

Day 41

Abide

"I am the true vine, and my Father is the gardener."

— John 15:1

John 15 says that abiding in Him is very important. We cannot do this without Him. We must be connected to His plan and purpose for our lives.

I haven't always abided in God. I was lost, hurt and lonely. I tried to pick up things he had taken away and believe me, it was most miserable. When God's Word says to no longer be conformed to this world but be transformed by renewing of your mind – that's exactly what He means. Let Go and let God. Abide and stay connected to bear fruit and prosper in Him. By not being connected because I wanted to go back to wordly ways, I was totally lost, and nothing worked my way. Nothing grew and no healings took place. I wanted to trust in my own thoughts, in my way or no way. It didn't work. I am glad He never left me. He remained when I didn't remain in Him. But God…

Spending time with God may seem hard for some and come easy for others. As we know, when it's time to read His word, sometimes we get tired or distracted by everyday things in our lives. We never find the time until something happens. We need to put on the whole armor of God and be strong in the Lord and in His promises. Unless we abide in Him, we are not connected. Being connected is being in His word and having that relationship with Him, following His commandments and meditating on His word. By remaining attached to Him as our source of life, we will produce fruit. God is the true vine and He takes care of His branches (true believers) in order for them bear fruit. Those who don't bear fruit are the branches that are no longer abiding. They no longer have a relationship or connection with God.

God has an individual plan for each of us and if we go to Him and abide in His word, we will have that divine connection. Follow the Word for yourself and try not to do what someone else does or try to become what someone else is.

My day includes prayer, intercessory prayer, worship, and praising Him. There are days I fast as well as pray. Being like that tree planted by rivers of water that bring forth fruit in its season. Being able to read and study His word I consider to be a gift from Him.

By reading my bible, studying His word, and fellowshipping with the people of God in bible study, at church, and other social gatherings, we become strong in the Lord. Every day my time is different and by spending time with Him my relationship in Him is strong. Just allow God to direct your paths and lean not unto your own understanding. The branches that God prunes will become more fruitful and He will remove anything that diverts or hinders their relationship with him.

Day 41 _____

Scripture and Notes

Day 42

Don't Give Up

"Show me thy ways, O Lord, teach me thy paths."

— Psalm 25:4

We must ask God to show us His ways and teach us daily what He want us to know. We must thirst to know God's ways and know something about God's acts. Some know who God is and have heard of the miracles that He has performed but don't really know Him personally. We must humbly submit our ways to God and commit ourselves to godly living. He will show us and teach us the way we should go. When we go through our situations we must so desire to want to be led into the righteous ways and in the truth of His holy Word.

Your situation may be a little tough right now, and your circumstances may seem like they are uncontrollable, but don't give up! Regain your territory and stop allowing the devil to steal from you. If necessary, take your city little by little. Joshua said to the people, "Shout, for the Lord says to take the city and do it on the seventh day" (Joshua 6:16). So, don't give up but allow God to direct your paths. When you pass through the waters, I will be with you, they will not overtake you. When you walk through the fire it will not burn you (Isaiah 43:2). Whatever you may be facing or may be experiencing in your life—I am here to encourage you to get through it and to never give up! It is easy to let go and give up! It is easy to say "I QUIT"—it takes a little faith to get through it. Philippians 4:13 reminded me that I can do all things through Christ who gives me the strength. God has plans for me according to Jeremiah 29:11 so I needed to hold on and seek Him for my plans.

There have been so many times I felt like throwing in the towel on everything. I felt like giving up at school, quitting my business, and just sitting and having that pity party. But there was this still small voice inside of me telling me to P.U.S.H. (Pray Until Something Happens). And that is what I did. I followed the direction of the Lord and continued to pray over my circumstances until a change came. I now have my master's degree and other certifications because of it. I am working on my business and meeting new clients daily. I am so thankful for all that He is doing. God opens doors and makes ways we cannot see. So, don't give up. Let God's promises shine on your problems because everything God is preparing for you will be worth the wait.

Just remember He will show us His ways and lead and guide us into all truth. Just know we must have that relationship with Him.

Day 42 _____

Scripture and Notes

Day 43

The Empty Nest

"Weeping may endure for a night but joy cometh in the morning."

— *Psalm 30:5*

What is an empty nest? The term Empty Nest Syndrome refers to feelings of sadness or an emptiness one feels when children grow up and leave home. This condition affects both parents, but it is more often experienced by mothers. While many parents experience a sense of loss and distress, it can also be a time when you focus on taking control of your personal needs instead of those of your children.

Why am I saying this now? My house has been empty for years. The children have all grown up and now have their own children. I am leaving my house of 19 years and it is bittersweet. It is an emptiness; I feel as if I am leaving something behind. Maybe it's the memories. The many times I gave my children spankings in those bedrooms. The crying at night as I would go through my storms. The times my husband nursed me when I had surgery and taught me how to walk again in my living room. The crying from the pain in life and healing in my bedroom. I think about all the fun we had and games we played and birthday parties we had for all the children. The many nights I rocked them to sleep when they were sick. The daycare and all the children we had in that house. The transition that took place may have been hard, but it was necessary.

Yes, it's my own empty nest. I was feeling like I was leaving those memories behind, but the truth is I am taking them with me. The sadness of leaving that home will not compare to what lies ahead. God reminded me that the memories are pictures etched into your heart. Those are for me and to hold onto for the rest of my life. There were times when our lives felt so empty and as if there was nothing to look forward to as we tried to find our way without the kids and came to a new land where God would make a way in our wilderness. We began to do things and find things in our lives we had never experienced before because it had always been filled with kids and no alone time for us.

If you are struggling, try to look at your empty nest as an opportunity for something new in your life. Know that God has a plan and purpose for your lives. It may look empty, but it is really a full nest. It is filled with joy and lots of love. We are enjoying all the new things that God has promised us. It is springing up and we are excited about everything He has done. God is true to His word. It was hard for me to let go and leave my first big house full of so many memories of hurt, pain, laughter and lots of praying. God gave it to us. That was the first big house we ever owned after we had section 8 and many rental properties. The devil says no. God blesses with a yes and something bigger than before, and then He opens doors. Yes, we struggled in life, but the struggle is over, and God has been doing great things.

Day 43 _____

Scripture and Notes

Day 44

A New Attitude

"Behold I will do a new thing now and it will spring forth, shall ye not know it? I will make a water in the wilderness and rivers in the desert."

— Isaiah 43:19

God says He is going to do a new thing, and that means brand new. It is something that has never taken place before and it will be a fresh new thing. I am excited about the new chapter in our lives and to know that it's something that has never taken place before, nor has it been discovered before in our lives. He told us to forget the former things and to let go and allow Him to take charge because He would bring us out of our wilderness. He would bring us to a place that we had never seen before, and we needed a fresh start. He would bless us and make our names great. So, we packed up and moved.

My husband and I moved to a place called Wilson, NC. Transitioning was hard and letting go of things was even harder. For the first time, it was only the two of us. He began a new thing in our relationship. By going through our empty nest years, My husband and I reconnected and discovered things we can pursue together. God took the emptiness I felt and gave me fullness.

God said He would do a new thing and He did just that. Doing a new thing means we would move to a new level of freedom and unity as we have never felt before. He is opening doors for my business and making a way for my husband to retire peacefully. He said that He would put water in our wilderness (those rejected, abandoned and uncultivated places) and rivers in our desert. And it will spring forth (leap out) and wou will know He did it. He said when we pass through troubles or face afflictions that He will be right there with us and will never leave nor forsake us. God has a future and a hope for us. So, we must walk it out in obedience and faith.

God has blessed me to write several books and journals since being here. I have a T-shirt store and a gift store, and I'm blessed with many powerful praying women in my Women's Bible Study group. My husband has a great Bible Study group as well. We are soaring for God and winning for the Kingdom. God has blessed us with a powerful church and a wonderful pastor. So great things are happening in our New. We are walking strictly by faith and not by what we see. He told us that He would make our name great and that we would be blessed, and we see that He has kept his word and is still keeping it.

Day 44 _____

Scripture and Notes

_____
_____
_____
_____
_____
_____
_____
_____
_____
_____
_____
_____
_____
_____
_____
_____
_____
_____
_____
_____
_____
_____
_____
_____
_____
_____
_____
_____
_____
_____

Day 45

Don't Be Discouraged

"Have I not commanded you? Be strong and courageous. Do not be afraid; do not be discouraged, for the LORD your God will be with you wherever you go."

— Joshua 1:9

Be strong and courageous. God will be with you wherever you go. You can choose to be strong and courageous even when you are feeling very weak. However, the weaker you feel, the more effort it takes to be strong. It all depends on your faith. If you continue to look at your problems and not at God, your courage will melt away. The choice to be strong rests on your confidence and trust in God. He will not leave nor forsake you. Look through eyes of faith and know that God will always be there. In the strongest of storms, He will carry you through.

Discouragement is one of the most troubling problems Christians encounter. It sometimes attacks without warning. Llike bone-chilling cold weather, it almost paralyzes us to the point where we feel like quitting.

When everything seems to be going wrong, refuse to get discouraged and refuse to give up.

Remember that God often surprises us with His love and great and amazing gifts. I am never limited by the way things are or by the things that we cannot see. Satan will try to separate us from our family and friends of the faith, but it won't work. Joshua 1:8- Be strong and courageous. We will endure if we continue to trust God. He is extremely creative and most powerful. With God all things are possible! Matthew 19:26 (KJV)"But Jesus beheld them, and said unto them, with men this is impossible; but with God all things are possible." There are no impossibilities. The longer you wait for your prayers to be met, the closer you are to your breakthrough. Meanwhile, wait on Him and trust His plan. Discouragement is one of Satan's favorite tactics to keep us from achieving our many victories.

Fear and discouragement are natural when someone has experienced setbacks and failures in life. God, however, gives us His word that He will be with us and He will help us to get through our fears and setbacks. So, don't give up or get discouraged. Wherever you are at this moment, and whatever you may be going through, just know tomorrow will be better than today and God will surely be with you.

Day 45 _____

Scripture and Notes

_____
_____
_____
_____
_____
_____
_____
_____
_____
_____
_____
_____
_____
_____
_____
_____
_____
_____
_____
_____
_____
_____
_____
_____
_____
_____
_____
_____
_____

Day 46

Trust Him

Faith is defined as belief with strong conviction; firm belief in something for which there may be no tangible proof; complete trust, confidence, reliance, or devotion. Faith is the opposite of doubt.

Webster's New World College Dictionary defines faith as "unquestioning belief that does not require proof or evidence, unquestioning belief in God, religious tenets.

"Trust in the Lord with all thine heart and lean not unto thine own understanding."

— *Proverbs 3:5*

In all our ways, activities, and decisions, we should acknowledge God. We must live daily in that trusting and close relationship with God. We should always look to Him for direction when making decisions.

When God promised Abraham and Sarah that they would be having a baby, they were both very old. They were put in an impossible situation. Abraham's faith didn't become weak, but he probably thought to himself, how am I going to do this, Sarah and I both are so old, but God promised. Some things in our lives seem so impossible but with God all things are possible (Matthew 19:26). Abraham simply took God at His word and went on. Sarah, on the other hand, decided that she was too old, so she thought it was ridiculous and laughed. But Abraham stood still and trusted God in it all. Whenever a situation seems almost impossible, the word of God says to lift our eyes to the hills from where our help comes (Psalm 121:1-2). Family, friends, wealth are only temporary and should never be viewed as our ultimate source of help for life. God is our only source of help in life. He is the only one who can meet our needs physically, spiritually, mentally and emotionally. Therefore, we must trust Him with all our hearts and lean not unto our own understanding (Proverbs 3:5-6) We must seek Him for every plan and direction because He will always help us in the time of need.

Whatever your situation may be, even if its seems impossible, just know that God is able to do it. It may be your marriage, your children, finances, or maybe you think that the things in your past are too hard to get through. Just remember that God deals with the things that seem so impossible. Don't worry. If you pray and then you worry it will not work and you will find yourself still in that situation. Worry is like a rocking chair-- it just goes back and forth and doesn't move. We don't need to know what God is doing or if He is going to do it, all we need to do is trust Him in all our situations. He will do whatever He says in His Word. All things are possible to those that believe.

Day 46 _____

Scripture and Notes

Day 47

God will Fight for You

Exodus 14:1 says The Lord will fight for you, and you shall hold your peace. Our God is an all-powerful God and an awesome God. He wants us to call on Him for all things, when times are good and when they are seemingly bad. I talked about the importance of resting, and this is a place where that rest is vital. When you really feel at a loss for what to do and you're running things over repeatedly in your mind, it is probably time to call on Him! Ask God to come down and fight for you! There have been many times when I have prayed and prayed and haven't been able to get that 'breakthrough' so I just say, "Lord, I don't know what to do anymore. I have prayed for this situation to be resolved and right now I am feeling lost and stuck. I feel like just spinning my wheels here. I just need you to come down and fight for me. I know in Exodus you say that I can call on You and You will fight for me. I thank you for doing that right now Father. In Jesus name, amen." After we have called on Him to fight for us, we need to be in His rest. Rest is a huge part of our inheritance. Before Jesus came to the Earth to suffer and die on the cross, God's people had no rest. But death could not hold Him, the grave could not keep Him from rising again for you and I. God's children, who were constantly having to earn their way into God's heart with their works, who lived under the law, now lived under the new covenant of grace, as we still do today! Probably the most important part of resting is that while we are resting we are to be praising God, giving Him all the glory, and to be in Thanksgiving with Him for the things that we know He is doing in our lives. We should praise Him for things that have not even happened yet but because of our faith in Him, we know they will happen. When you are weathering the storms in life, don't forget to call on God. There is no limit to how many times you can call on Him.He wants all your problems–big and small. Talk to Him, commune with Him daily. Let Him into your world like you never have before because the truth is, He wants to come down and fight for you and all you have to do is call on Him, and He will fight for you.

Day 47 _____

Scripture and Notes

Day 48

Show Me your Ways

"Show me your ways, LORD, teach me your paths. Guide me in your truth and teach me, for you are God my Savior, and my hope is in you all day long."

— Psalms 25:4-5

God is the only one who can lead and guide us . We must be willing to always seek His guidance and His direction in everything. It is not enough that we understand His ways, but God will lead and guide us as we read His word. Psalm 86:11 says Teach me your way, LORD, that I may rely on your faithfulness; give me an undivided heart, that I may fear your name. We can pray "Father, please teach me (show me or explain to me) and help me to understand the direction in whichyou are leading me. As I journey through Your Word, I find the direction that You are taking me in that day. I see that You keep Your promises as I trust You with my life's issues. Sometimes we have things we go through that may be tough and it may seem as if we can't get them under control , and we need to seek You for that divine direction. Show (make obvious; demonstrate it) me your ways Lord and lead and guide me unto all truth as I know You can." We must let God's promises shine on our problems and understand that sometimes God is preparing us for that waiting season. Because change isn't giving up; doing nothing is giving up. Just know as God is teaching us what we need to know, we must be humble enough to follow the direction He has set before us. To show me your ways means that we are willing to walk in obedience of His word, that we are willing to develop a prayer life and other spiritual disciplines. It means that we are willing to pray and wait on the Lord, and that we will be teachable so we can grow in God's truth. To walk in God's way is to walk in spiritually and to grow and develop in His truth. It means to fear Him, to trust Him, to seek Him continually and to obey Him. We must humbly submit to Him and commit ourselves to living godly lives. We must fear the Lord as a child of the most High God and we should fervently pray to know His ways, His heart, His purpose ,His Wisdom and mostly live by His Holy principles. Through the suffering of Christ we come to know God Himself.

Some of us know what God can do and have heard of His many miracles, and we know that He can give peace in the middle of a storm and yet do not have a close relationship with Him. Our daily prayer should be, "Lord show us your ways and lead and guide us in your truth, so that we can walk the plan and purpose that You are calling us to. Help us to have that relationship with you that is needed in order to live victoriously.

Day 48 _____

Scripture and Notes

Day 49

Be Still and Know

"Be still, and know that I am God; I will be exalted among the nations, I will be exalted in the earth." The LORD Almighty is with us; the God of Jacob is our fortress."

— Psalms 46:10-11

Be still. This is a call for those involved in the war of your marriage, addictions, even bitterness to stop fighting, to be still. The word still is a translation of the Hebrew word rapa, meaning "to slacken, let down, or cease. We need to stand firm on God's promises and let go. Exodus 14:14 says to be still and God will fight for you. Give that battle and addiction to God and let Him handle it.

We do not have to move at all, but stand in faith and know that God is able to heal, deliver and set us free from those things that come to kill us, steal from us, and destroy us. Being still means if we trust Him and have faith that He will bring us out of the storms to where we can stand firm on His promises. God said He will supply all our needs and send that great Comforter to lead and guide us into all truth.

We all must let go and make decisions about our life and the situations that we are living in. We need to allow God to take over. When we let go of our ego and get out of the way, God can do that immediately. It's like the man at the pool of Bethesda who was waiting on people to help him. He was paralyzed and couldn't help himself in the pool at the time of the stirring of the water, so he lost hope. He lost faith until Jesus came and asked him one question," What do you want"? He said, "I want to be made whole. But no one will put me in the pool." Jesus said "Arise, take up your mat and walk" and Immediately he got up out of that situation and walked. He was now fre of those troubles that had been carried with him on that bed for 38 years. He was now in control of his situation. In that bed was affliction, hurts, pains, anxieties, his childhood, bitterness and some abuse. That bed was heavy, and he was carrying it for all those years. God is the only one who can free us as long as we have the faith to know that He can do it. This man needed to "Be still." He needed to let go and quit holding onto things that would keep him bound. We all have those things -- bitterness, hurts, unforgiveness, generational issues, maybe a bad relationship. These things keep us from exhalating God and allowing Him to have His proper place in our lives.

We can't always depend on people; we must depend on God for our immediate response. If you are purpose-minded, you will get rid of those ego trips and pride and stop allowing it to keep you from your destiny. Arise, take that bed up and walk. You have been stuck too long. Let it go.

Day 49 _____

Scripture and Notes

Day 50

Focus Forward

"I do not claim that I have already succeeded or have already become perfect. I keep striving to win the prize for which Christ Jesus has already won me to himself. Of course, my friends, I really do not think that I have already won it; the one thing I do, however, is to forget what is behind me and do my best to reach what is ahead. So, I run straight toward the goal to win the prize, which is God's call through Christ Jesus to the life above."

— Philippians 3:12-14

If you have been feeling miserable because of things in your life or your past, just know that discouragement is the exact opposite of courage. When you feel discouraged and you have lost motivation, press **forward**. (Make up for lost time; pick up speed; proceed forward; progress; push on). I encourage you to change your focus and shift in a new direction. Have the determination that you are going to be what God has called you to be to have all that God has given you and to receive all God died for you to have and more.

So, when you feel discouraged—FOCUS FORWARD. Speak to yourself and say, "I will not live in this bondage ever again. I am forgetting those things that are behind and I and moving forward to those things that are before me. I will enjoy my life and have the promises God has promised me to have. I will release the past things in my life and go on pursuing what God has for me this day forward."

Day 50 _____

Scripture and Notes

About the Author

Lorraine Jones-Whitfield is the wife of an Army Veteran Elder Carlton Whitfield Sr. Lorraine is dedicated to helping people live according to God's Word and to walk in the purpose that God has called them. Lorraine is a Christian Family Counselor, Christian Life Coach, and Teacher. She mentors and consults in marriage and family and children's ministry. She is the CEO of Hannah's Heart Ministry and S.H.E Soars LLC. Women have been blessed by Lorraine's online S.H.E Soars LLC ministry and the family and marriage ministry, and her ability to lead and guide hurting women by equipping, educating, encouraging and empowering. This is done through the word of God and other resources such as women's prayer breakfast, Women's Empowerment and Transformational sessions, AIT (Anointed Individual Training) Military style Boot Camps, and in helping them W.I.N (Walk In New) and to Find their IDE-NITY in live and the Lord.

Lorraine and her husband, Carlton, are parents of seven and grandparents of 15 grandchildren and have been married for over 38 years and now reside in Wilson, NC, where they work in the ministry and have a powerful marriage and family counseling group together. Carlton is a pastor and is currently mentoring and instructing in God's Word with an awesome online ministry and home-based bible study group. They love to meet people where they are and reach them for God's glory.

Lorraine is available to speak at women's events, retreats, fellowships and more.

Connect with Lorraine

• www.lorrainejoneswhitfield.com
• https://www.shesoarsllc.com
• https://www.facebook.com/Lorraine.Whitfield
• email: hannahsheart7@gmail.com

18 Powerful Scriptures
on Faith that will move mountains.

"But without faith it is impossible to please Him, for he who comes to God must believe that He is, and that He is a rewarder of those who diligently seek Him." — Hebrews 11:6

"Behold, his soul is puffed up; it is not upright within him, but the righteous shall live by his faith." — Habakkuk 2:4

"But Jesus turned him about, and when he saw her, he said, Daughter, be of good comfort; thy faith hath made thee whole. And the woman was made whole from that hour." — Matthew 9:22

"He said to them, "Because of your little faith. For truly, I say to you, if you have faith like a grain of mustard seed, you will say to this mountain, 'Move from here to there,' and it will move, and nothing will be impossible for you." — Matthew 17:20

"And all things, whatsoever ye shall ask in prayer, believing, ye shall receive." — Matthew 21:22

"And if Christ has not been raised, then our preaching is in vain and your faith is in vain." — 1 Corinthians 15:14

"Therefore, since we have been justified by faith, we have peace with God through our Lord Jesus Christ." — Romans 5:1

"For I am not ashamed of the gospel, for it is the power of God for salvation to everyone who believes, to the Jew first and also to the Greek." — Romans 1:16

"So faith comes from hearing, and hearing through the word of Christ." — Romans 10:17

"Having gifts that differ according to the grace given to us, let us use them: if prophecy, in proportion to our faith." — Romans 12:6

"For we walk by faith, not by sight." — 2 Corinthians 5:7

"Yet we know that a person is not justified by works of the law but through faith in Jesus Christ, so we also have believed in Christ Jesus, in order to be justified by faith in Christ and not by works of the law, because by works of the law no one will be justified." — Galatians 2:16

"So then, those who are of faith are blessed along with Abraham, the man of faith." — Galatians 3:9

"For by grace you have been saved through faith. And this is not your own doing; it is the gift of God," — Ephesians 2:8

"In all circumstances take up the shield of faith, with which you can extinguish all the flaming darts of the evil one." — Ephesians 6:16

"But as for you, O man of God, flee these things. Pursue righteousness, godliness, faith, love, steadfastness, gentleness." — Timothy 6:11

"By faith we understand that the universe was created by the word of God, so that what is seen was not made out of things that are visible." — Hebrews 11:3

"And the prayer of faith will save the one who is sick, and the Lord will raise him up. And if he has committed sins, he will be forgiven." — James 5:15

These scriptures on faith show us that through faith we are made righteous with God, we can please God and we become His child, we can be healed and can receive the very spirit of God into our hearts. With faith we can be used by God as vessels to do His will. — Unknown

Made in the USA
Middletown, DE
05 September 2020